When I S̶a̶w̶ ̶Y̶o̶u̶  T0083030

Carolin Emcke

When I Say Yes

Translated by Tony Crawford

polity

Polity Press
65 Bridge Street
Cambridge CB2 1UR, UK

Polity Press
101 Station Landing
Suite 300
Medford, MA 02155, USA

ISBN-13: 978-1-5095-4087-7
ISBN-13: 978-1-5095-4088-4 – paperback

A catalogue record for this book is available from the British Library.

Typeset in 12.5 on 15 pt Adobe Garamond by Servis Filmsetting Ltd, Stockport, Cheshire
Printed and bound in Great Britain by TJ International Ltd, Padstow, Cornwall

The publisher has used its best endeavours to ensure that the URLs for external websites referred to in this book are correct and active at the time of going to press. However, the publisher has no responsibility for the websites and can make no guarantee that a site will remain live or that the content is or will remain appropriate.

Every effort has been made to trace all copyright holders, but if any have been overlooked the publisher will be pleased to include any necessary credits in any subsequent reprint or edition.

For further information on Polity, visit our website: politybooks.com

This text is based on a stage performance
which premiered at the Schaubühne, Berlin,
in December 2018.

You and I apart are easier to limit.
– Kate Tempest, 'Tunnel Vision'

Speaking about the nature of writing always
includes speaking about the nature of speaking;
it is a bridge to the second person, the third,
the other.
– Enis Maci, *Eiscafé Europa*

Acknowledgements

I thank everyone, acquaintances and strangers, who have attended my solo evening *Ja heißt ja und ...* at the Schaubühne in Berlin.

To be able to experience in the theatre what it's possible to set in motion by speaking about these issues, what is moving, what is disturbing, what is funny – has been both instructive and delightful.

I thank everyone who has told me afterwards, in letters or in conversation, about their own experiences: that has been a precious gift.

And it has changed my writing in this book.

ACKNOWLEDGEMENTS

I thank not least the whole team at the Schaubühne, whose generosity, loving attention to detail, and ginger tea have made it all possible.

In the beginning is doubt.

Before every sentence, every word, there is this threshold: Is that right? How do you know it's true? It is fair? Besides being true, is it also truthful?

And those are just the doubts about *what* I might say.

I write as if I were mumbling: softly, more to myself than aloud for others to hear. Thinking, rather, but with a keyboard. Writing makes thinking more precise. It's intimate. Like whispering. Or like mumbling. Maybe that's why I always write barefoot. As if, with my feet in shoes, I would only be able to think in conventions.

The moment I imagine an audience, everything dissolves, and immediately I am silenced. Objections step in front of my own ideas and

upstage them. To say nothing of the antago-
nisms, the raging animosities. They scare me;
they get under my skin, like poison; I can feel it
spreading in my body, all over; feel it paralysing
me – my voice, my will, my self.

In the beginning is always doubt.
Sometimes I wish I could turn it off. But, if I did,
the *I* of my writing would not be me. It is in writing that I find myself, invent myself.

* * *

In my childhood, when there was no way to avoid
mentioning the supposedly unmentionable, it
was hinted at by a word in dialect. *Mitschnacker*
was a word in Plattdeutsch, the Low German of
the flat, northern country, and even children who
didn't know any Plattdeutsch sensed the word's
sinister connotation. 'Don't let any *mitschnacker*
get you': that's what they said to us on our way
out into the world – to school or to the sports
field. It indicated the danger, but indirectly. As
if the dialect could cushion what it was we had to
be warned about. We were not to talk to anyone
who tried any *mitschnacken* – that is, who tried
to talk to us and gain our trust. But what would

happen if a stranger did talk us into going with them – that was left unspoken.

And we left it unquestioned; we don't question it even today.

What can happen, what did happen, time and again, what happened to generations of girls and women before us, what still happens to girls and women – not only, but mostly – all over the world, on the way to school, on the way to fetch water, on the way to the pasture, on the way home – what they can do to us: that is not stated. Our mothers and grandmothers before us were informed the same way: without the information. No one told us we could be manipulated, lied to, picked up, picked on, attacked, abducted, in a car, in the bushes, in the woods, in a shack, in a basement; no one said we might be raped, choked, injured and killed. And most certainly no one ever said the danger lay not only outside, among strangers, but also, and most often, close at hand, in our own homes, in our own families.

'Don't let any *mitschnacker* get you.'

That's a farce. It sounds funny. As if it were merely about someone who talks too much. But what it means is not the talking; it's the danger of violence after the talking.

It's these rhetorical disguises that facilitate what they claim to prevent. Incredible: supposedly they're warning you about something, but *what* it might be, they don't say. It's not just rose-tinting, because that would mean denying there was anything you had to be warned about. It's leaving unspoken what someone might do to you. As if it were indecent to talk about it – suppressing all mention of it instead of suppressing the act itself.

Thus there is a taboo, not against the criminal act, but against naming it. Right from the start. Thus the convention undermines not the person who perpetrates violence but the people who want to tell us about it. The suppression of speech shifts the onus of justification. It's the person who wants to speak out about something unmentionable who feels wrong or dirty. That is where the complicity lies.

In order to criticize something, you have to be able, and willing, to imagine it. In order to imagine something, you have to be able to name it. If violence is kept abstract, if there are no concrete words for it or descriptions of it, that keeps it unimaginable,
implausible,
untouchable.

*   *   *

The bathrobe.
I just can't get over the bathrobe.
Everywhere in the #MeToo stories, this bathrobe keeps turning up ...
Not at the beach on holiday. Not in the bedroom at home. But at a meeting in the office. At a meeting in a hotel. In what purports to be a professional context.

What is this obsession with the bathrobe?

I don't get it. I really don't understand it. I simply don't understand the scene. What's happening in it. What the *point* of it is. No one ever explains it. Not in the situation itself, and certainly not after the fact. You have to think it all through yourself.

Young women, older women, co-workers, employees, hotel staff, interns; women these men have been working with for some time, or complete strangers; women who expect to see a man in a suit, in jeans, in whatever clothes, but in any case *dressed* – women are called in, and then:
ta-daaaaah,
the bathrobe scene.

I picture this in my mind's eye all the time. The only bathrobes I can imagine are white terry cloth. I have no idea why. And yet guys like that probably wear silk ... what do I know? I've been hearing these stories so long, it's interfering with my relationship to my *own* bathrobe.

Answering the door in a bathrobe – what's that about? Is it the prologue to an anticipated conquest? Is it an invitation to sex? Is it pride? Look what a fabulous dick I have? Do they honestly believe that? A woman goes to a meeting and, before she knows it, out of the blue, a dick walks up to her? That could be the opening of a joke. Like the psychiatrist jokes people used to tell: 'So this patient comes in dragging a toothbrush on a string.' Only this joke starts differently:

'A dick walks into the office wearing a bathrobe ...'

Is that supposed to afford pleasure? And, if so, to whom? What kind of pleasure does it give the dick's owner? Pleasure in humiliation?

He's not exhibiting his naked body, he's parading his ability to control: his ability to suspend all propriety (in a work context), his ability to dominate, to humiliate, at a whim, whenever he feels like it. If it's not appropriate to the situation, so much the better; if it goes against all convention, against what's customary in a meeting, against what ordinarily makes up desire: mutual pleasure and tenderness, passion and devotion to another.

The bathrobe is always out of place.

So far, there is *not one* story in which the bathrobe turns up in a way that is harmless or appropriate or seductive. *No* story in which a couple want to throw something on after a night of passion, *no* story in which a man wants to arouse a woman, one woman wants to arouse another, a woman wants to arouse a man by letting themselves be looked at, revealing themselves, surrendering themselves to the gaze of another, with a bathrobe on at first, then without. No story in which the bathrobe conceals something that is then revealed slowly, the wearer's nakedness, the wearer's vulnerable physicality.

The bathrobe is always out of place.

Clashes with the context. The situation. Is neither erotic nor practical nor pretty.

And yet we often hear: 'Well, what did she expect? Goes to a meeting in a hotel room – how naive can you get?'

In a work context, a man asks a subordinate or dependent woman to meet him. It may be in an office or in some other place. In industries where work is mobile, where people have to travel to different cities to meet with co-workers and contractors, it very often may be a hotel room that has been booked for appointments and meetings. A man asks a woman to meet him there, a woman who knows she is less protected because she's less senior, less known, less connected, less visible, less audible; because she's a woman; perhaps unsure because she has never been alone with a revered or even just a famous professor, a priest, a producer, because as the housekeeper she's responsible for the cleanliness of the hotel room or the offices, because as the nurse she's responsible for the patient, because as a police officer or a soldier she's subordinate to a superior, because she's wearing a headscarf,

because, because, because, ...

because she doesn't know what to expect.

After all, how is a person supposed to expect *that*?

Is it naive to expect *not* to be humiliated?

Is it wrong to expect *not* to be harassed, attacked, injured, choked? Is it naive *not* to expect to have your head beaten against the wall, *not* to expect to be dragged across the floor by your hair, pulled into the bathroom, penetrated by force; is it wrong *not* to expect to be pissed on and tormented? Is it really so naive to expect *not* to be raped?

What kind of logic is that? What kind of concept of humanity? What kind of concept of *men*? As a woman, must I accept that it's unrealistic *not* to be seen and treated as an object, as a thing, as an available, usable body?

What kind of idea is that: that people should go through life anticipating every moment that they are going to be another person's object? How should parents teach that to their children? How have generations of mothers (or fathers) taught it? What a responsibility: all parents would like their children to go through life without fear, to feel safe and free, but at the same time they don't want their daughters (or sons) to grow up naive about what others see in them or what others want to do to them. Generations have grown up with this indistinct knowledge of their own vulnerability – and we carry that with us through life.

When I had been with my first employer for just a few weeks, I received a call on the office phone from the publisher. That was unusual. He was rarely seen in the editorial offices. But he did have a word to say from time to time, and occasionally he turned up in person. Timidly, I took the receiver, expecting to be criticized or corrected.

Instead, there was a jolly gentleman on the line full of praise for a story I had written. After I rang off, I turned around, and half the department was standing in the doorway of my office, waiting to hear what he had wanted. Before I could explain, my editor said, 'If he's asked you to meet him at home, I'm going with you. You're not going there alone.'

I *hadn't* been asked to meet him at his home. But the stories of young staff writers who had been summoned to meet with the publisher, who then received them in his bathrobe, were notorious. How many women had had to go there alone before my time, I don't know. Nor do I know what happened. That was passed over in silence. What the silence concealed, I can only guess. But I do know that my editor was certain I would need his company.

There was also an older editor who placed orders with the cafeteria to lure waitresses to his office, where they arrived to find him masturbating. The editors and staff writers, almost exclusively male, told each other and me this story with mixed amusement and disgust. But it didn't occur to any of them to tell their wanking colleague that his behaviour was offensive. No one wanted to take responsibility – not even those who said they had once heard a shocked young woman run out of the office screaming. The horror came to an end one day when the waitresses' boss delivered the order herself and told the editor in no uncertain terms that he had to stop. In my time there, I did not observe such scenes. I only heard the story told. That was grim enough.

The story was congruous with an atmosphere in which women had to decide, over and over again, whether to treat each transgression as harmless, funny and flirtatious, or as demeaning, humiliating and terrifying. I can't say I've always been able to tell them apart, for myself or for others. In retrospect, I wish I had been more autonomous in some situations. In retrospect I can think of moments when I *wanted* to perceive as harmless something that was actually embarrassing. Why did I laugh it off? Today I can't quite say. We probably tend to gloss over embarrassing experiences because we don't like to be embarrassed. And that makes it difficult after the fact to describe our own experiences honestly. Because then we would have to admit that what we tolerated wasn't really pleasant even at the time. To criticize it after the fact, we would probably have to admit to having been more chicken-hearted than we like to think. We would probably have to admit that the casual, friendly atmosphere among our co-workers perhaps wasn't always so casual. We would have to admit that there were probably others who got hung out to dry, who could have done with more support, more protection.

And, most importantly, as a homosexual woman, I had the advantage of a sad misunderstanding: that is, of being perceived by male colleagues as an equal – but as male. Men have treated me with special respect, particularly in offices where the atmosphere was misogynistic. They disparaged me less than other women – because they didn't perceive me as a 'real' woman in the first place. That was a relief and a strain at the same time. As I was integrated in the community as an androgynous 'one of the guys', my status rose in accordance with the community's values: machismo outweighed homophobia. Situations like that were much

more bitter for gay male colleagues, who were
denied what I was granted unasked: that highly
prized masculinity.
The preconceptions were equally wrong in both
cases.

But maybe that was also the reason why I never
got invited to the publisher's house and greeted
by him in his bathrobe.

*　*　*

I try to make visible the layer, or, as modern tech-
nicians say, the interface, between knowledge and
power, between truth and power.
That is the problem I work on.... I don't have a general theory, nor do I have a reliable instrument. I feel
my way; I build instruments as well as I can to make
objects visible.

– Michel Foucault, 'Power and Knowledge'[1]

What does that mean, 'power'?
It's so wonderfully imprecise.
As if everyone knew what power is.
As if it were perfectly clear who has it, what it
consists of. As if it were a static thing.

What substance, what kind of material is this power to abuse made of? The power to overstep boundaries, the power that exceeds its limits, interferes in the rights, the shame, the bodies of those without power? Is it made of different stuff than the power to behave benevolently? Is it only an excess that makes the difference, or is it a different substance, a different use, a different relation?

Power is usually described as an instrument of domination:
one that can be localized, focused, personalized;
power as repressive and vertical, pressing downwards;
power as an instrument that serves the purposes, the will, the pleasure of an authority;
power as the power of a person, a gender, a class, an exclusive caste;
power as negative power
to suppress, hinder, manipulate, use, injure, destroy,
without fear, without retribution, without consequences;
the power of the producer; the power of the land-owner; the power of the department head; the

power of the theatre director, of the priest; the power of the shift foreman. The power to break other people's needs, wishes, dignity; the power to humiliate, insult, shout at, touch, talk over, embarrass, harass, molest, torment; the power to eliminate, dismiss, exclude; the power to deny recognition, cap pay, cast roles, close doors.

That is both correct and oversimplified.
That is the conception of power that leads to slogans like that of the French #MeToo discourse: '*Balance ton porc*' – 'Squeal on your pig.'
Good grief . . .
It's hard to decide which word is the least apt, but it's clear which one is the most disastrous: the 'your'. That word once again inscribes the injurious experience in the victim's own subjectivity – not only the crime but the perpetrator too is attributed to the victim: 'my' perpetrator, 'my' rapist, 'my' assaulter.
'Wounded attachments' is the name coined for this connection to one's own injury by the political theorist Wendy Brown.[2] And that is exactly the bond that has to be broken, the attachment we want to be released and freed from: the grip of power.

There is also the power of charisma: power through closeness, power through experience, through knowledge, through an aura; power that elicits admiration and is in turn validated by admiration.

That may be the form of power that is least understood, and the form that is so easily dismissed in public discourse.

People ask without thinking: 'But why didn't she resist?' 'But why didn't he say no?'

That shows a failure to recognize the contingency, and the ambivalence, that relations of power or powerlessness can have. A failure to recognize that powerlessness can be associated not just with fear but also with love and affection.

An Afghan woman who has fled to Britain together with her husband, who has no assured residence status, who speaks no English, who lives in a strange city with no one she can trust, feels defenceless in her social isolation against the beatings of her husband, the only person to whom she has any relationship at all.

An elderly woman who would never leave her home, her room, her bed, if it weren't for her caregiver, who brings her meals and washes her, feels defenceless and at this person's mercy when they sexually abuse her.

A schoolgirl who wants to meet her fellow students' expectations, who wants to be accepted just like everyone else, a schoolgirl who wants to be included in the parties, the drinking, doesn't want to be thought uncool, immature, timid, is afraid to stand up to the group of students who sexually assault her. She may not even know exactly what her will would be, because no one gave her time to form it, because they slipped her knockout drops, because they made videos and later blackmailed her with them, because ...

A schoolboy who wants to meet his fellow students' expectations, who wants to be accepted just like everyone else, a student who doesn't want to join in the parties, the drinking, but doesn't want to be thought timid, 'unmanly', 'gay', is afraid to bail out of his fellow students' game, which has ceased to be playful and become harassing and assaulting.

A doctoral candidate working under an admired professor whose texts he reveres, whose charisma awes him, doesn't want to repulse her when she harasses him, not only because she can make or break his career, but also perhaps because his fear is mixed with disbelief that such a wise person could so egoistically overstep all the boundaries of professionalism and responsibility.

There ought to be a phenomenology of the emotional dependencies that get lost in the all too vague conception of power as domination. Emotional dependencies exist not only in clearly hierarchical relationships; there are also other ways in which constellations of power can bind, can curtail freedom, can shape or mould actions.

Power comes in many forms. It can also exist as an unplaceable, omnipresent, intangible power. The productive power that also creates the subjects it oppresses,
a power with no centre, strategic, but with no individual strategist behind it.
The power that operates through concepts and codes,

the power of memory, and the power of silence that is handed down from generation to generation,
the power of denying what a family wants to repress, what a society wants to negate,
the power of practices and habits that have solidified so naturally into social habitus that they are no longer thought about,
the power of contempt for precarious classes who are so disparaged that they are not even named,
the power of stigmas that are no longer declared but cast in the social grammar itself, persisting as implicit connotations,
the power of images and patterns in advertising, in films, in video games, in music that shape our perception of what and who we consider valuable or valueless.

This is the power that sways the decision as to who is credible and who is not, whose abuse is funny and acceptable, whose harassment is their own fault and harmless, part of the business model, part of the workplace culture; this is the power that sways the decision as to who dares to speak up, who rejects the shame or the ascribed portion of guilt for their own humiliation; this is the power that sways the decision as to who gets help, who is heard, who gets protection, for whom circles of silence are broken, the decision as to what skin colour, what clothes, what status, what femininity is more deserving of protection than another.

It is the productive, creative power which doesn't just destroy but also produces: the dynamic, multifarious power that creates images and self-images, not once, but over and over again; the power that inscribes itself not only in bodies and gestures but in feelings and beliefs, in implicit knowledge, in verbal and non-verbal habits.

That is the power we have to think of and change.

'I don't have a general theory' to make it visible, 'nor do I have a reliable instrument.'

Maybe that's why I'm writing in this odd, indeterminate form, in miniatures and fragments on power and equality; maybe the only way I can is by searching, switching genres, now narrative, now analytical. Maybe my writing needs this aspect of work-in-progress so that it can also be understood as an invitation to think together. Maybe that's why, for the first time, I'm writing something to be spoken aloud first, a text that has to work orally. Maybe because these questions still leave me unsure, because I'm not always certain of my own intuitions, because I too of course have been permeated by all the old images and conventions, because I know how precarious, how fragile all certainties are when they have to prove themselves in dialogue with others. But mainly because I believe that emancipation movements often begin with the stories we tell each other, with the gentle, quiet, careful conversation among friends, among family, in relationships, with one other person, or with several.

We have to feel our way forward and try out instruments with which we can question our practices and beliefs. For me, that meant writing something in a different, hybrid form: more vulnerable, insecure, open.

*   *   *

I didn't see the actual blow.

The blow with which the husband punished his wife, disciplined her, shamed her; the blow with which the husband injured his wife; the blow that struck her skin, her face, her head, her assumptions; the blow that wasn't the first and won't have been the last, the blow that broke down their relationship before their relationship broke down, the blow that destroyed what Jean Améry once called trust in the world, her trust that she was safe from attack, the blow that inflicted violence on a loved one, the blow that struck the woman while the baby was in the same room, the blow that the baby must have heard –

that blow changed:

from an act of violence – from an act the man performed – into something that somehow allegedly performed him ...

The blow, whose trace I could see in the woman's face, has now, retroactively, not injured the woman; now the blow is apparently a blow that struck him, the man, not her whom he struck; humiliated *him*, not her; the blow she suffered is now allegedly making him suffer, and not only that: the blow that was his is now not his, did not come from him, but from the circumstances, from something he can't control, something beyond him, who is now concerned mainly with himself, not with her, his wife, whom he struck in the face, so that now she doesn't want the blow, which struck her, to be *talked* about.

The blow was no longer the blow. The blow was the not-talking about the blow.

She doesn't say that. Not at first, in any case. She only shakes her head. Tears are running down her face, over the red patch that she can't shake off. The blow occurred in the other room. We had been invited to dinner. My friend, whom I will call Nadia, had invited me, along with two men I didn't know, to her and her husband's beautiful home. The food was delicious and we were glad to be there. But we were still on the starters when little digs appeared; Nadia's husband aimed barbs at her, at what she had cooked, jibes half restrained by social convention – and our presence. Or maybe our presence heightened his pleasure in sneering at her. Maybe we were the audience without which there would have been no point in sneering at her.

Maybe the pose of power needs an arena in which to exhibit itself. Little malicious violations. Maybe I should have said something right away. Maybe I should have expressed my discomfort. Instead of going along with Nadia and the others at the table, reinterpreting his disgusting behaviour as amusing by our strained laughter. Whose strain was I trying to relieve?

I had already abandoned her. I was *tolerating* the way he was demeaning her.

Why do we do that? Why aren't we able to stop right away? Why do we suppress our correct intuitive urge to name what we perceive as unacceptable or inappropriate? What mechanism keeps us quiet? What social forms, what timidity makes us make the wrong choice?

I suspect that we restrain ourselves in these situations because we don't want to cause a fuss, don't want to interrupt the pleasant progress of a nice evening. And yet, at that point, the evening *isn't* nice.

For the sake of pleasantness, we tolerate unpleasant humiliations.

For some reason, the burden is always shifted. The person who feels miserable or ill-mannered is the person who refuses to tolerate transgressions. The person who feels awkward is the one who speaks up about inappropriate behaviour.

How does that work? Why are the hostile little barbs, always pronounced in an ironic or casual tone, the deprecations of Nadia, still consistent with what is called a lovely, relaxing evening? Why would an objection to those jibes have been perceived as an inappropriate disruption?

Or would it not have been perceived as inappropriate? Is that perhaps just what we've been taught for generations: not to cause a fuss, to endure being demeaned, to tolerate and compensate for the 'moods', the abusive behaviour of others, to indulge them and avoid conflicts?

Or is it because an objection would have demeaned Nadia further? Was I waiting for her to defend herself? Would my speaking up have embarrassed her further by signalling that she needed someone to speak for her? Or is that just a clever excuse for cowardice?

We were sitting at the table. Nadia had gone into the next room to check on her husband and the baby. As best I can recall, the baby had cried and he had left the table to go and comfort it. When he had been away for some time, Nadia went to check on them. And was gone for a surprisingly long while. We talked, tried to fill the gap until one of our hosts reappeared. It was slightly embarrassing. We didn't know each other and were suddenly sitting here alone, without the people who had invited us.

One of the other guests said later that he had heard the blow. I hadn't. I only saw Nadia when she came back. She sat down in the same seat as before, played the role of the hostess as before, went on talking as before. She wanted to continue the evening, to pick up at the point where she had stood up and left the room; the interim, the time she had been in the next room, the time during which she had been struck by her lover, her husband, the father of her child – that interim was to be cut out and discarded. She wanted what had happened not to have happened; she didn't want to talk about it, as if talking about it would make it real, as if it would

27

no longer be possible to deny it once it had been pronounced.

She sat there, a smart, modern woman and a friend, with the tears running down her face. She didn't want to talk. She wanted to serve the next course. She didn't want to interrupt the programme. Didn't want to deviate from how she had imagined this evening, although the evening was no longer what we had imagined an evening could be.

Wasn't this something that couldn't happen any more in our generation? Weren't we young, self-assured, sophisticated, everything we had thought would guard us against having to respond to domestic violence?

Then Nadia and I went into the kitchen for a moment while the others stayed sitting at the table. In the kitchen we could talk. The kitchen as a safe space.
Cliché.
Only now do I notice how comical it is. The gay couple alone at the table, the wife-beating husband gone missing, the two women in the

kitchen. Preparing the next course as an opportunity to talk, between the familiar hand gestures, about the other person's hand.

I offered to do what seemed to me the best I could do: to take her and the baby home with me immediately. To put her up at my place. To go with her to see a lawyer. Anything but stay here. Anything but pretend nothing had happened. Anything but pretend it was all right, because it was not all right. Anything but gloss over with civilities what could not be glossed over.

All she wanted was for us to stay, not to leave, just to have dinner together and talk. As if nothing had happened.
We stayed.
Against our better judgement. What else could we do? We sat there across from each other and talked, I can't remember what about, something, something that could have been anything but what we *wanted* to talk about: the blow.
We sat there and played, out of love for our friend, a farce that was not funny; we sat there and hoped, minute by minute, for an ending. All

we wanted was to get out of there. Everything was wrong.

Her husband did not reappear, by the way. He stayed in the baby's room.

At last it was over.

I remember the moment when we, the guests, were standing outside the door, in the street – and didn't know which way to go. We had left her there. That was what she had wanted. We had been discharged into the night, ashamed of our role of having been witnesses and not intervened, having been witnesses and unable to act, accomplices to something we had never wanted to experience or tolerate: domestic violence.

Nadia went on living with her husband for years before they separated.

I was no longer close to her during that time. I couldn't do that: face her husband as if nothing had happened; look on as a friend while Nadia continued to be mistreated, while she couldn't find her way out of that relationship, while she looked for reasons why her husband was violent, or why he allegedly wasn't violent; why he just hit her, just sometimes; why ... there are reasons after reasons after reasons; in the attempt to rationalize their partner's violence, women – and men – produce mountains of reasons, yet they can never begin to fill the abyss of the irrational violence.

I am ashamed of not having stood by Nadia, and yet I suspect it saved me from the greater shame I would have felt if I had stood by her and had to look on.

A good friend I was not. A good friend would have stayed. No matter how miserable she felt. Maybe. Maybe not. I try to persuade myself that my refusal to see the violence as normal may have helped her in the end to see the violence ... as abnormal.

Maybe.

Maybe there is no 'right' in stories like this one. Maybe that's exactly what the violence accomplishes: it harms everyone, maims everyone, plunges everyone into a darkness that has no end until we exit the sphere of violence and run away.

And maybe not even then.

Those who have been in it recognize its approaching shadow.
Those who have been in it evade not only violence but also the microscopic hints that precede it. Those who have been in it can't stand hearing it glossed over, trivialized, whitewashed, justified, denied, repressed, infused with alleged reasons or good intentions.

At the time, I could think of only two possible reactions: take Nadia with me or leave her there, as she asked me to do.
But just to go into the room where her husband was hiding and speak to him, to confront him without mincing words – it's not that I was afraid to do that: I didn't think of it.
That didn't even occur to me.

P.S.:
In the three years ending in March 2017, 239 women were killed by their partner or ex-partner

in England and Wales. The women were stabbed, strangled, shot, drowned, beaten, burnt to death.[3] According to the Office for National Statistics' most recent 'Focus on Violent Crime', 80 per cent of women who were victims of homicide were killed in their own homes.[4]

According to the Crime Survey for England and Wales, an estimated 1,517,000 people were abused, coerced, stalked or threatened by their partner or ex-partner in the year ending in March 2016. Of that number, 1,028,000 were women – that is, 67 per cent.[5]

* * *

Clifford Geertz, citing the philosopher Gilbert Ryle, describes what is known as a *thick description*.[6] He uses the example of three boys who seem at first glance to be performing the same movement: all three boys are moving their right eyelid rapidly up and down. They are *blinking* one eye.

However, the first boy's blinking is an involuntary *twitching*. It's a nervous tic.

The second boy's blinking is a signal which he intends someone else to see. It is *winking*. The first boy's eyelid movement may be the same as the second boy's. There is no way to tell them apart just by looking at them. But the first boy's blinking is unintentional, uncontrolled, not directed at anyone.

The second boy's blinking, on the other hand, is intentional and directed to an addressee.

Only the winking is communicative, has a social meaning. There are cultural codes for winking: the receiver may feel he or she is being addressed in a certain way – conspiratorially.

The third boy now performs the same movement: he blinks his right eye. But he is mocking the first boy's movement; he is imitating the tic to make fun of it. Perhaps he has even practised his spiteful parody in front of the mirror.

Geertz uses this example to illustrate what he calls *thin* and *thick descriptions*. A thin description refers only to the perceptible action: the rapid up-and-down movement of the right eyelid. The thick description, on the other hand, includes the intention, the social context and the cultural codes, and interprets the action in the light of that information.

To talk about sexual harassment, abuse and assault, we need thick descriptions.

An isolated gesture doesn't tell us anything. There is no way to judge, to revolt, to condemn – if a description names nothing but an isolated action. A media shorthand which mentions only 'touching' makes no sense. It has no more meaning than 'the rapid up-and-down movement of one eyelid'.

'Touching' per se is nothing but a contact between one person's body and another's. It may refer to putting a hand on a leg, an arm, a buttock. And without a further description of the intention, the context, the addressee, without an understanding of the codes and rites that obtain in a given social situation, in a given culture, there is no way to interpret it. The hand movement can arise from joy, silliness, familiarity; it can be perceived by both persons in a given situation as playful, passionate, arousing. It can also occur as inappropriate, intrusive, condescending, molesting, and can be so perceived by one or both persons. The same hand movement indicates something different in the dark room of a club among strangers than in a bedroom between lovers, and something else again in the office between co-workers in hierarchically unequal positions.

Many of the controversies about the #MeToo movement originate in an exchange of thick and thin descriptions. Usually a person, a man or a woman, tells a story, describes a very specific experience at a specific place, in a cultural, social, historical context in which he or she is inappropriately, abusively fondled with a movement which is referred to as 'touching'.

The critics who react to such stories dismiss them with thin descriptions. They say it's 'ridiculous'; 'touching' is harmless; 'flirting' becomes impossible if 'touching' is no longer allowed. The whole discussion, they say, promotes a 'puritanical' culture.

In other words, the critics respond to a description of a very specific abusive touching (the mocking wink) by talking about a neutral 'touching' (the twitching eyelid). And sometimes a specific thick description is countered with a quite different thick description – as if one could be a rebuttal to the other.

'All these details.'

I can already hear the objections to thick descriptions.

'Do all these embarrassing scenes have to be thrashed out in detail? What good does that do?'

It does good in several respects. Without the details, it is hard to judge the credibility of a statement. Without thick descriptions, there is no way to assess what exactly happened, what the abuse consisted of, whether it was a come-on, a harassment, an assault, whether it was exploiting a position of power, or something else. Without the specific scenes, there is no way to look for clues that would allow us to receive a story as plausible or implausible. If we want to be fair, want to make precise distinctions, don't want to demonize sexual acts per se, we need thick descriptions.

The drawback of thick descriptions?

They supply us, initially, only with *individual cases* and, what's worse, they supply individual cases in a richness of detail and in an explicitness that some people find obscene, others superfluous, and others again petty, and in some cases it is exactly that.

For people who *don't* want to think about relations of power, who *don't* want to think about ideological underpinnings, *don't* want to think about the social, political, economic conditions that facilitate, encourage, shield such behaviour in individual cases – for them, thick descriptions are a dream. Because, on the face of it, a thick description explains the misbehaviour only in one individual case, in a specific situation. There are no conclusions to be drawn from that. It has no consequences. No one has to think about their own thinking, their own routines, their own conduct, their own ways of behaving or talking.

Those who would criticize sexual abuse, assault and harassment as socially or politically tolerated practices must always examine whether they can demonstrate and argue *both* a specific case with a thick description (and possibly another, comparable specific case, and another) *and* the structural similarities or differences, the ideological assumptions, the discursive and non-discursive practices that normalize abuse and violence.

Sometimes there are no conclusions at all to be drawn from an individual case. Not every case is typical, symptomatic, generalizable.

And sometimes a structural critique is too general, too abstract: too much political assertion, not enough specific demonstration.

For those who *do* want to discuss the issues of abuse of power and sexualized violence, not just legally, in reference to specific cases, but also as matters of social policy, culture and ideology, it's not easy to find a genre that can be precise and at the same time fair; concrete and at the same time political.

*   *   *

What do *I* have to say? Or, to put the question another way: Who am I to say anything?

Those who reject homosexual desire as perverse, unnatural, sick, and even those who consider themselves 'tolerant', often deny homosexual men their masculinity and homosexual women their femininity.
The diversity of physicalities, the multitude of

variations, of gestures, the diversity of ways to be female or male or somewhere

in between,
in motion,
else –

that diversity is blanked out again and again by distorting images and concepts.

And those images and concepts have always excluded someone like me,
even as a child: left me out.
They didn't fit. They still don't fit.
It's not that *I* don't fit within the norms: the norms are not fitting in regard to me.
Something has always been too short or too long, too heavy or too light; usually too unambiguous.

I don't like monochrome.

There are predefined thresholds and boundaries that dislocate a person, take a person out of a territory, or keep them from entering it. Forever outside. Not that this outside feels wrong. It's as if this state of exile were a place in itself, always displaced, elsewhere, and yet exactly right; acting out my pleasure, desire, sexuality, with friends (boy- and girl-) who are also at home in this movable elsewhere – I had no word for it when I was growing up; later I didn't want a word for it, because that, it seemed to me, would inevitably come with a new set of restrictions. Would inevitably come with the same kinds of norms and codes that I would again have found unfitting or unwanted – static, not dynamic.

Maybe that's why the term 'queer' says it best, less as an adjective, more as a verb, to *queer*, or to *queer something*: to subvert, thwart, baffle, frustrate, make a mess of something. The part that essentializes, congeals into identities, tries *yet again* to define rules, conditions, 'real' and 'fake', 'authentic' and 'inauthentic' – I always make a mess of that. Not with any ill intent. It happens all by itself.

In any case, I can anticipate being denied competence to say anything at all about #MeToo, because as a queer person I'm not supposed to have a female perspective.

As if ignoring, patronizing, harassing women did not involve *me*. As if I had no experience of the various forms of misogynous contempt or machismo.

That is one of the reasons – reasons that are not easy to admit – why I have been hesitant to contribute to this discussion, why I tell myself I first have to show why I might have a right to speak. In this way I have already let myself be denied the female perspective. As if I couldn't speak as both a subject and an object of desire.

This question contains another embedded in it – and perhaps one that concerns me even more acutely: What difference does my own identity make in my ability to identify or empathize with others?

The public discourse occasionally assumes a person must be a member of a certain group, must have had a certain experience, to be able to understand that experience and speak about it.

Is that the case? Can only those people who have experienced social injury, racist discrimination, sexual abuse, talk about it? What would that mean for the social discourse? What would it mean for my own writing, which is concerned mainly with the experiences of other people, in other countries, other contexts, other life-worlds?

In the present debate, two different assumptions come up.

The first assumption is:
Other people's experiences are not accessible to our examination, not *understandable*.
Is that true? Really?

Naturally it's *easier* for a person who fulfils the norm to think norms make no difference.
Naturally it's easier
for those who are perceived in a society as belonging;
naturally it is easier
for those who never get asked by police for their ID,
for those who get asked to show their ticket in the train only once, and not over and over again;
for those who always receive an answer to their letter of application,

43

for those who don't get brushed off by estate agents,
for those who get admitted by bouncers in clubs,
for those who are always addressed explicitly in all government forms,
for those who don't have to work their way from one office to another, from one form to the next;
for those who can eat whatever they feel like, because they can afford it;
for those who find characters in films who look like them;
for those who don't systematically turn up in song lyrics as weaklings or perverts,
for those who are perceived as individuals – and not just as a member of a group, as a representative of a culture;
for those who are perceived not as an identity, but as a person,
it is easier
to think there is no discrimination.
Because it's not part of their own everyday experience.

But that doesn't mean a person can't examine and understand what it means to be discriminated against. Discrimination can be understood abstractly, as structures and mechanisms of exclusion, but it can also be understood quite concretely when someone tells us about it.

To relate to other people's experience, all I need is the knowledge *that not everyone looks, lives, believes, loves the same way I do*.
I need the awareness that the conditions of my own existence are *not generalizable*.
I need the willingness to learn something.

To learn from others what they experience, and not to dismiss their stories out of hand as implausible – just because they never happen to me. I need only the simple curiosity to listen to what the everyday experience of non-white or non-Christian or unemployed people, or even just *women*, is like.

However, that also means that, conversely, we who are more vulnerable in *certain* respects, who perhaps have *somewhat* more experience of violence, of contempt, of derision or exclusion, have to understand that it is *not* part of other people's everyday experience; that what is a day-to-day experience for us is astounding to other people when they hear about the pain and the sadness that are as much a part of our lives as our happiness; that we have to *explain* it, patiently, over and over again.

We often perceive other people's hesitation and amazement as distrust or rejection. We react with resentment because it seems unimaginable to us that other people still can't imagine our day-to-day experiences.
That's what *we* have to learn.
To be more patient.
Not to automatically equate not knowing with not wanting to know.
That is tedious. Some days – no, many days – we don't have the strength for it. It wears us down.
But it's necessary if we want to achieve change.

That is what I had written until the advent of the *#MeTwo* movement, the public recounting of experiences of discrimination in Germany that followed Mesut Özil's resignation from the national football team.[7] Until exactly that tedious narration of excluding, racializing, painful experiences was met – not only, but in many cases – with massive rejection.

When migrants, people of colour, Muslims, Jews began sharing the degradations they encounter every day with us white Germans who have no immigration in our family history, when they did *not* generalize but described exemplary individual experiences –
many simply didn't believe them;
many accused them of whining or ostracizing;
many dismissed their experiences as fantasies, as vanity, as over-sensitivity, as ingratitude.

I don't know if I would write again today what I had written before that: that the people who have more experience of marginalization and exclusion in various ways really need to be so patient. Whether they really must or can find the strength to explain those experiences. Whether it isn't sometimes too much to ask. Whether they don't have the right to say sometimes, 'I'm tired of this. I'm sick of this.'

The second assumption is:
Perhaps people can understand the experiences of others, but they *shouldn't* comment on them.

That is disastrous.

A person who has never been sexually harassed themselves, a person who has not been demeaned or humiliated, a person who does *not* know such feelings from their own experience, ought to be allowed to talk about them too. Structural inequality and asymmetric relations of power can also be criticized by those who are not personally disadvantaged by them.

Those who have been granted privilege and status – by birth, by belonging to a certain class, culture, nation – can question those privileges. Perhaps it is not so easy to notice or to identify the injustices when they are not inscribed in one's body every day in the form of specific acts of ostracism. But that doesn't mean one can't understand them and criticize them. Even without personal experience, we can identify and criticize the structures and logics of exclusion and inclusion, of belonging and non-belonging, of equality and inequality.

Why shouldn't white people be allowed to talk about structural racism, heterosexuals talk about homophobia, atheists talk about freedom of religion, men talk about sexism? In fact, I expect it of them.

Not a day passes on which I don't think: 'Please, can't someone else explain this today?' Not a day on which I'm not ashamed that it is once again left to Jews to talk about anti-Semitism, left to Muslims to defend the headscarf as *one* possible religious practice, et cetera.

Without the ability and opportunity to think beyond our own needs, beyond our own group, class, form of life, without developing concepts and comparisons between different experiences, there is no way to think of justice, recognition, freedom.

A discourse in which each person is allowed to artic-ulate only their own needs, their own perspectives, their own interests, is mutilated, is just a sequen-tially collective monophony.

We need the diversity of voices and experiences: to reflect on our own positions and then adopt other perspectives, to set ourselves in relation to others and to the structures in which each of us is situated. This happens constantly, if we are honest, because we are never situated in just one position, never in just one context, never in just one configuration of power. We are always located in several very different hierarchies and constellations at once. There are different experiences of discrimination, and they overlap, but so do privileges, and so there are also shifting alliances; we have shifting experiences in common with and shifting differences from each individual person.

To me it is absolutely necessary to throw light on these different relations, over and over again. To reflect on the ways in which I am tremendously protected and privileged. Spared much that people in other regions of the world, or other people who live near me but in different sets of social or cultural relations, have to deal with. To remain conscious of what an undeserved fortuity it is to be able to live and work the way I do; to remember humbly that my social position protects me from experiences that others are burdened with, every day.

And yet there are also, *at the same time*, those respects and contexts in which the experience of exclusion, of hatred, of menace is mercilessly inscribed in me, in every fibre of my body; ways in which laws, texts, practices, in Germany and also in countless other countries in the world, mark me as other, criminalize me; ways in which my loftily promised human dignity is still up for negotiation, every day. Even at home; not only in faraway places. But to criticize practices and structures of exclusion, I don't have to be the victim of them myself.

Inequality will not be abolished unless those who benefit from it join in criticizing it.

Being allowed to speak, to express criticism, against a practice or a structure that excludes others, not myself, doesn't mean always *having to do so*, having to have the first or the last word.

It's not self-censorship, but decency and tact that demand we let others speak first, listen to others first, engage with their self-descriptions and stories, and refer to them. If certain voices and perspectives have been marginalized historically, then those persons and perspectives must be allowed to be the authors of their history – and not repressed by speaking 'for them'. But it can be our task to clear space for that discourse, to open it, to use our position to make the narratives of others more audible, more visible.

So why am I speaking here? As who?

The position from which I am speaking is that of someone who loves and desires, who loves and desires *women*, who looks at women and is looked at by women. This position could be relevant because I speak, potentially, as someone who looks at, thinks of, desires women as sexual counterparts and, at the same time, looks, thinks, desires *as* a woman. It could also be relevant simply because a person is looking, thinking, desiring.

* * *

In 2001 I was in Afghanistan with the photographer Thomas Grabka. In Kabul. The American troops and their allies from the Northern Alliance had captured the city. 'Liberated' it from the Taliban, they said at the time. On one of the first days, we discovered a small building a little way apart from the old royal palace with a group of Northern Alliance militiamen standing outside it. 'The National Museum,' one of them explained; their improbable duty was to guard it against destruction. We talked with the soldiers and they invited us into their tiny guardhouse for tea. We sat on the carpet and were served by a boy.

His age was hard to estimate. His hands were those of someone used to working with his hands, used to working hard; I could imagine that those hands knew how to care for animals, how to guide a plough, how to build a hut. Now those hands put the kettle on, brewed the tea, served it. He was so quiet that his whole form seemed to dissolve; he was present, but with no presence. When he had served us, he disappeared into a side room, where he squatted down and began patching a soldier's uniform jacket with those hands.

Naim, as I will call the boy, was a 'private prisoner' of the Northern Alliance, kidnapped from Pakistan, dragged along through the war, not as a child soldier but as a slave, expected to do everything, ordered to do everything that seemed to be needed. We could not find out how long he had been captive and transported along with the troops; what would become of him now that the war was ending (that's what we all thought then, at least); whether he would ever be set free, whether he would ever be able to live his own life, whether he would be able to go back home – all of that was unknown.

For years I thought about this captive, sewing boy. For years I wondered what kind of life that was, how lonely, how hopeless, how sad. For years I wondered whether they liberated him; every time I read about the liberation of girls, about education for girls, I thought of this boy in this guardhouse.

And then one day, years later, I read an article about Pakistani boys who were kidnapped and taken to Afghanistan where they were kept as slaves; I read that 'warlords' or militiamen often kept boys not only as domestic servants but as all-purpose objects, as thralls who were often abused, raped, assaulted. I read more and learned of the old tradition of the *bacha bazi*, the 'boys' play', for which pubescent boys, *bacha*, were trained to dance in women's clothes for entertainment at parties (and sometimes for sexualized use). There were countless ways in which boys could end up in this role. Some parents may have given them up voluntarily, but some indentured their sons to pay off debts.[8] I suspect Naim was too old for a *bacha*. But not for everything else.

I remember feeling dizzy as I read these stories. I thought of Naim. I had forgotten his name in the meantime. But not his face. I searched through all my files from trips to the Middle East. I wrote to the photographer and asked whether he remembered this sad boy in the little guardhouse in Kabul, whether he could look for a photo in his archives.

© *Thomas Grabka*

I stared at the picture, saw this boy, and only now did I imagine what he may have experienced.
Only now did my imagination fill in what a taboo had blanked out: the fact that boys too can be victims of sexualized violence. That those regimes or those men who claim to be strictly heterosexual, who pathologize and criminalize homosexuals, can abuse not only girls and women but also boys and young men. Only now was I able to imagine clearly what had been unimaginable before. Only now did I add more possible experiences to my perception of the captive boy.

I don't know what happened to him. I don't know what has been done to Naim. I only know that I had eliminated and denied what *could* have happened to him because I couldn't even *think* it.

Perceptions do not just happen.

What we perceive as fact is the result of a dynamic, selective process. There is a distinction to be made between 'perceiving' something (*percipere*) and 'being aware' of something (*appercipere*). We admit sensory perceptions, filter them, structure them, organize them in contexts and remember them; we compare perceptions with our previously stored knowledge, interpret them according to the available concepts and chains of association – until we become 'aware' of them, consciously understand and accept them.

Because the ability to perceive something has to do with what we have perceived before, because new knowledge and understanding arise in relation to what we already know or have understood, it is difficult for information that contradicts our interpretations of earlier experiences to find acceptance. We disqualify what we have never heard before as unheard of; we are more likely to interpret it as implausible than information that readily replays old knowledge.

We can be sorry about that, or we can seize it as a challenge and an opportunity to learn, to change, to act.

If perception (and understanding) has something to do with *quantity*, that is, with the *frequency of an experience*, then we can practise perception. Both as individuals and as a society. Imagining something, imagining yourself in a situation or empathizing with someone, accepting that certain experiences or occurrences are possible: these get easier the more often we try them.

That is what matters to me in many of the #MeToo stories. Not the accusations or the essentialist assignment of attributes to men or women, but the different perceptions and different ways of perceiving. Expanding our imagination, imagining what we would rather not think about, what we would rather not think possible. Changing our way of looking at one another, making it more free, more reciprocal, more just.

Perceptions don't just change by themselves. It takes repetition. Like all learning. We have to practise hearing and listening, seeing and looking, until we are ready to perceive something else besides what the taboos and conventions would dictate. We have to practise new perspectives until they gradually replace the old reflexes of seeing and thinking what we wanted to see, wanted to think.

For some, that may result in not *just* Muslim men, not *just* refugees being *visible* as perpetrators of sexualized violence, but also Christian men of

European backgrounds. For others, it may result in refugees *too* being visible as perpetrators of sexualized violence. In this way both the ones and the others will have shifted their internal images closer to the external realities – and perhaps qualified some of their resentment-soaked fantasies.

For some, it will result in not just women occurring as victims and not just heterosexual men as perpetrators.

For some, it will mean thinking about women's day-to-day situations in the first place, about their working conditions, their salaries, the expectations they are supposed to fulfil.
For some, it will mean perceiving those people who otherwise tend to be forgotten or overlooked. For some, it will mean thinking about other people's perspectives for the first time.

But when our perception changes, when the way in which we talk about power relations changes, when we question the guidelines that define who is untouchable, when our certainties change, when we stop maintaining the circles of silence – then new possibilities become imaginable for those who didn't dare defend themselves or speak up before.

That too is something we can learn, individually and collectively: not to think ourselves powerless. For some, that will begin with feeling less isolated. For some, the story of someone else who had the same experience will help them to overcome their fear or their shame; they will feel that they don't have to shield their partners or their mothers or their siblings, that what seemed too embarrassing, too sad, too painful is something that can be shared; they will discover that there are places or forums, people or groups who listen to them, who respect them, who believe them; they will feel invited to speak among their friends, in their families, at their workplaces, in court – and in this way reinforce their sense of strength, of autonomy.

That's not easy. It makes no sense to expect that everyone will be equally able to do it: to stand up for themselves so easily, to tell their story so easily. I am often surprised at the rigidity with which some women in comfortable circumstances say it should be expected of everyone: to protest, to speak out about what they don't like or what has happened to them, to resist every assault and every degradation. I am afraid they fail to consider all those historical experiences that have shaped older women in particular (but not only them), and they also disregard the cultural differences in the education of girls and boys, deny all the social conditions that make it easier for some people and harder for others to articulate their own wishes and needs.

Instead of deriding or disparaging those who are less daring, we should be creating a social climate in which they are better able to understand and articulate their experiences.

* * *

It can't be true.
At first, there is only resistance. Next they say they are 'appalled', 'astonished' and, most of all, 'shocked'. In their initial reactions to the news of crimes committed, people often express surprise that such an act, an offence that violates their moral expectations, is possible at all.
It can't be true.
Experiences of abuse and violence intrude into a life that up to then was secure. They not only

61

hurt and injure those who suffer such experiences: they also disturb those who hear or read about them.

The implicit hope is that the evil that human beings are capable of will remain the exception. We can't understand how a person could do that to another.

It can't be true.

Shaking their heads in disbelief is a reaction of self-defence on the part of those who are not the victims. We can't live in constant mistrust of our fellow human beings. We can't live with the expectation that every other person is capable of assaulting or attacking us at any moment.

In this respect, offences and crimes are not just a moral problem but also a *cognitive* one: they are difficult to understand because they do not have a place in our practised expectations of the world and other people. They can only elicit incomprehension.

And so there is an intuitive explanation for the initial reactions to all the different cases in which a person faces investigation or trial for sexual assault or harassment. The public shock expresses not only moral indignation at an intolerable act but also the mutual reassurance that this is something out of the ordinary, something that must not be seen under any circumstances as the usual state of affairs.

It mustn't be true.

There is something *reassuring* about such a declaration of social abhorrence. It affirms a consensus about standards of human interaction. A world in which every mistreatment and every act of violence was taken for granted would not be a world we would want to live in. It is quite a different matter, however, when someone is not just morally irritated or disturbed by such an act but pronounces it unthinkable or impossible because the person accused of the act doesn't seem like a *classic perpetrator*.

When the act supposedly can't have happened, because the person who is suspected has up to now been a harmless neighbour or a respectable citizen. Such resistance is all the more curious when it comes with the explanation that this or that person who is under accusation is a dedicated activist or a good friend, that their extraordinary artistic or educational or political achievements speak for themselves.

The idea that someone who is likeable or gifted cannot have committed a crime is absurd. There is no evidence to indicate that only people with evil written all over their faces tend to commit crimes, or that people who play Schubert sonatas or develop security features for computer programs or recite Hölderlin poems never mistreat, abuse or assault anyone. An internationally renowned professor of philosophy is just as capable of unbridled assault as a less renowned night-school teacher of consumer affairs.

Up to now, there are no indications that *any* talent – in fine arts, in mathematics or even in friendship – can prevent a person from humiliating, abusing or tormenting another in a given situation. Intelligence or general niceness does not preclude a capacity for sexual abuse and brutality.

The converse is also true, however: even the dumbest, most narcissistic slimebucket can be *innocent*. Just because a person has all kinds of annoying qualities and eccentric habits – that doesn't prove anything. The readiness to think some people capable of sexual abuse just because they live a wild life, because we never did like them, is just as negligent as the readiness to defend certain people against even the most credible accusations just because they have a fascinating talent.

By the same token, there is no reason why the victim of a crime must be likeable or have a clean record. People with a less successful or a turbulent biography, people who have a previous conviction, can also be victims of sexualized violence. Just because someone is dependent on drugs or lives on the street or is merely grouchy and hard to get along with – that doesn't mean they can't have been wronged.

All that matters is the question whether a person has had something forced upon them, whether something was done to them against their will, whether they were free to consent or refuse without coercion. They may be in a relationship, they may be a chance acquaintance, they may have met in a bar or in a business meeting – that makes no difference. It may be impractical and confusing, but the images of people and the images of their offences are not *congruent*. A demonic act and its perpetrator need not resemble each other.[9]

* * *

We therefore reject efforts at the national and international levels to implement this ideology through such instruments as gender studies, quota rules, e.g. for the inclusion of women, propaganda campaigns such as 'Equal Pay Day' or 'gender-neutral language'.

The AfD wants the family policy of the federal and state governments to be oriented to the image of the family as father, mother and children. We reject all efforts to extend the sense of the word 'family' in Article 6, Paragraph 1, of the German Constitution to include other communities and to revoke the state's special protection of the family in this way.

– From the 2017 election programme of the AfD party[10]

Those who want to restrict freedom are not hiding their agenda. Those who recognize only a repressive concept of equality are organizing.

They are mobilizing
under various names and titles;
they are radicalizing, in Hungary and in Brazil, in Russia and in Turkey, in Italy and in Saudi Arabia, in the USA and in Germany; their anti-modern, obscurantist ambitions are undisguised;
they want to support only *some* women, foster only *some* families, recognize only a *certain*

66

concept of nation, only a *certain* religion; they discredit anything else as 'unnatural', 'foreign' or 'unhealthy', as 'elitist', as 'cosmopolitan'.

Some claim to be evangelical, some Islamist, some Russian Orthodox.

They appeal to a certain 'used to be', a time when the nation is supposed to have been imperial or homogeneous or God-fearing, before so much fuss was made about the separation of powers, before the Geneva Conventions were in force, before torturers were shamed; a time when the junta was still in power or the tsar or whatever undisputed, undemocratic authority, almost always masculine; an imagined, imaginary time when the traditional family was seen as a Christian or Islamic or somehow 'natural' constant, and not as a product of history; they tell different stories, have different historical references, but they all have in common their recourse to the authoritarian attitude that scorns civil rights and women's rights; they have in common their homophobia and transphobia, their racism, construing the Other to suit the society in question; they have in common their contempt for science, their ruthlessness, their mercilessness, their unwillingness to forgive – and they very often have in common a will to degrade and destroy ...

In that light, these are no minor issues, no trivial issues, no elitist issues.

For some women, for some men, for some trans persons in many countries in the world, for those who love differently, live differently, the issue is bare survival, saving their bare bodies from torture, imprisonment, mutilation, lynching.

For others, who are spared the worst,
for all of us,
the issue is the survival of freedom.

That is why feminist issues are not luxury issues. The discussion of abuse and sexualized violence, the criticism of structures of exploitation, of chauvinistic, homophobic and transphobic practices and beliefs – this is not a secondary, subordinate discussion to be taken up after the primary, important, real problems have been addressed and solved – those of the workers, those of the unemployed, those of the people who have been socially marginalized.

The logic of 'principal concerns' that must be taken seriously and 'secondary concerns' that can be postponed, belittled, put aside is contemptuous because It sets up a hierarchy of pain.

The pain of these people is supposed to be more important than the pain of those 'other' people?
Oh, right –
and the other people's pain, the secondary, not so urgent, negligible pain, always just happens to be the Black, the gay, the female, the Jewish, the migrant pain.

That has to stop.
'There is no hierarchy of oppressions,' the American poet and civil rights activist Audre Lorde once wrote. There is no priority that dictates whose human rights and whose civil rights need to be enforced first. There is not the social need of the majority on the one hand and the cultural need of the minority on the other. Not to mention how amusing it is to see women counted as a minority yet again in this equation.

Respect is not something you have to be able to afford; respect is not something that can be postponed.
Respect is due. Always.

Issues of recognition *are* social issues and redistribution issues. And vice versa.

It is false to pretend people could be divided in this way. It is wrong to pretend there are no Turkish women factory workers or gay Muslims or Jewish pensioners or ...
It is false to simplify the diverse, overlapping, mutually attenuating or amplifying experiences of belonging and not-belonging – just to resist the accompanying demands.

The discussion of abuse and sexualized violence, the debates on equal pay and equal representation, the issues of gender discrimination, quotas for women, and the concepts and images in which people think and talk about bodies and sexuality, the social, aesthetic, economic, political conditions which help to reproduce the disparagement of certain forms of life –

70

all of this is urgent. And it does not prevent us from reflecting on liberty and equality in other respects.

I can criticize ruthless housing policy *and* sexist language.
I can protest against exploitative working conditions in factories in free-trade zones *and* advocate the introduction of unisex toilets.
I can demand higher inheritance taxes *and* defend Muslim women's autonomy.
I can want a European unemployment benefit *and* sustainable climate protection.
I can also demand spaces for promiscuous sex practices, by the way, and at the same time approve of religious education in public schools.
Just to make the confusion *really* complete.

I can link social and cultural issues,
political and economic issues,
ecological and religious issues,
just as I can think of local issues in connection with global issues.

The polarities are false; they are aimed at disrupting the public discourse.

We mustn't allow ourselves to be played against one another. We mustn't be fooled into dividing ourselves into our white part and our gay part, or our migrant part and our atheist part, or our Black part and our middle-class part.

We must not deny our complexity, our individuality, just to fit into false monochromatic categories.

These are issues of freedom *and* justice, social *and* political issues, issues of the so-called majority *and* the so-called minorities.
They concern everyone in a democratic society.

*   *   *

'Puritanical witch hunt'.
At first I thought they had got something backwards. Or else the phrase had been cut out of a different article, was lurking on some clipboard, and ended up in the wrong text, the wrong context.
It happens.
Words get kidnapped, get used against their will, against their sense; they get abducted, unseen, unheard, and then suddenly they turn up somewhere else.

Oh!

Suddenly there they are, with no idea what they're doing there; they're in a strange neighbourhood where they've never been, where they don't know anyone, where they don't fit in or get along, like something standing in the way, blocking the view, a diversion, making people take a detour or stumble into an ambush.

At first I wanted to push the phrase back, show it where to go, tell it to go back where it belongs. But by then it was already in the world, being used, exploited.

'Puritanical witch hunt'.
How on earth is the term 'puritanical witch hunt' related to descriptions of sexual harassment and assault?
Why are feminist positions regularly accused of being a 'witch hunt', being 'puritanical', being 'rigorist'?
What do 'witches' have to do with anything? Or 'puritans', for that matter?
Seriously.

A woman or a man or a trans person describes how they were molested, harassed, abused, and the answer to that is: 'Puritanical witch hunt'? What puritan is hunting what witch? A person tells of an encounter, an experience, in which someone pressured them, harassed and upset them – and that spreads an atmosphere of terror? In whom?

The people who talk about a 'puritanical witch hunt' are those who are bothered by the public discourse, those who want to see the field of pleasure, of sexuality – the field of *their* pleasure and *their* sexuality – as a kind of unmentionable zone. As if their gestures and actions were above criticism. As if what gives them pleasure must be held unquestionable, untouchable.

And, at the same time, those who talk about a 'puritanical witch hunt' can take pleasure in anything; they can be amused by whatever they find amusing; they can lust for whatever they want to lust for – but they cannot choose what pleases or arouses others.

Strangely, pleasure is supposed to be *always* pleasure, even if it is unpleasant to a given person.

Pleasure is supposed to be always pleasure, even when it is all on one side; pleasure is allegedly always wordless, unconditional and above doubt – as if there were anything that takes place between two people that is wordless, unconditional and above all doubt.

That is perhaps the most interesting aspect of this 'witch hunt' reflex: that the critics claim to be easy-going and relaxed,
that they pretend to be castigating the other side for being uptight, anti-pleasure, 'puritanical',
while they want primarily to protect themselves, to castigate themselves, to repress themselves into an attitude which they *claim* is healthy and free in regard to their own sexuality, but which mainly maintains a taboo against talking about it.

Those who cry 'puritanical' are trying to prevent a conversation about what gives them pleasure by claiming that the other side is trying to combat pleasure and sexuality. Those who cry 'witch hunt' don't want to accept that there can be pleasurable touching and less pleasurable touching.

Someone merely says, 'What you're saying or doing, what you call pleasurable – to you – gives me no enjoyment, makes me afraid, shames me, humiliates me, hurts me.'

Someone merely says what she or he doesn't want.

That has nothing to do with puritanism; it has to do with *autonomy*.

Maybe the part about wanting needs to be explained again.

Not wanting *something specific* from a certain person does *not* mean never wanting *anything*.

Saying 'no' to a certain person or a certain act, gesture, practice does not mean there could not be a broad range of acts, gestures, practices that we would want, desire, say 'yes' to with another person, or even with the same person. A 'no' delineates only what the speaker doesn't want, in order, possibly, to open up spaces for what they do want, what gives them pleasure.

A 'no' excludes something, but it only draws a boundary that must not be crossed – this side of the boundary is open, free for fantasies, for experiments, for the pleasure of discovery and invention, together, searching, testing, uncertain and attentive, playful or passionate, with dildos or plugs, anonymous or familiar, hasty and hurried or slow and hesitant, with precise signals as in SM practices, no matter how different the touches and movements may be that give pleasure to one person or the other, always concerned with mutual pleasure, with consent to the mutual experiences that are possible, with a 'yes' that unambiguously means 'yes', from which it is possible to create, experiment, develop, experience something.

'Yes' is only the beginning: everything that comes after it, the 'yes, and ...', is undefined, is dependent once more on what each person wants. That is what's enchanting, alive, exciting; that's where it is – the pleasure that is coupled with curiosity, with unknowing; that's it – the pleasure that searches for a common language of the bodies, the gestures and the words; that pleasure can be explosive, radical, slow, fast, wild, tender, strong – but it arises only from assent, from the 'yes, and ...'.

It doesn't matter whether the sexuality is understandable from outside; whether it's pretty or not, whether it looks well-behaved or boring or disturbed; it matters only whether all the participants have been able to consent.

'Puritanical witch hunt'?

Why wouldn't it be interesting to hear what does or doesn't give pleasure to others? Why wouldn't it be helpful to ask that?
Of course it's possible we might make some unexpected discoveries.
We might discover that what seemed up to now to be consensually pleasurable, to be mutually amusing, playful, flirtatious, erotic, is not at all so to another person.
We might suddenly be embarrassed about what seemed up to now to be cool or harmless. We might discover challenges to our self-image. We might have to re-evalute certain habits that up to now seemed easy and innocuous.

Do I understand the perplexity that can result from that?
Yes. Absolutely. It *is* unsettling not to know whether another person understands our gestures, our words, the way we intended them.

Of course this is unsettlingly rough terrain; on every hand lurks the danger of striking the wrong tone, of being too quick, too late, too loud, too soft, too clumsy, too self-assured.

And yet – taking pleasure in the other person's pleasure is indispensable: enjoying uncertainty, discovery; talking to each other in all the erotic languages available. Whether that takes place in parks or in beds, in toilets or on sofas, whether it is private or semi-public, in chatrooms or in living rooms, whether the encounter is between strangers or longstanding partners, whether the pleasure and the practices are negotiated and agreed in advance, whether there is an agreed role to be played, or whether everything is undefined and yet to be discovered – what matters is mutual arousal, mutual enjoyment, mutual desire; what matters is what can grow out of mutual assent, out of a 'yes'.

That's just about the exact opposite of a 'puritanical witch hunt'. #MeToo is not about combating sexuality.

It's about taking pleasure in sexuality.

Abuse and assault are not sexuality.

They are abuse and assault.

Those who complain of a 'puritanical witch hunt' or a 'war on sex' are trying to shift the shame. Trying to ridicule as ashamed those who feel, not shame, but anger or grief or the desire for something different. That is too often forgotten: that the experience of humiliation and contempt not only makes people angry but also demoralizes them. Women who defend themselves are readily accused of rage without recognizing how deeply they are afflicted with grief and melancholy. That is why it is so important to tear down the shame and take back pleasure.

No one should be ashamed who has been abused or raped; no one who has been exploited and harassed, no one who has been unable to defend herself or himself, who has been paralysed with fear, able only to whimper or weep or keep silent; no one who has suffered violence, been accosted, shouted at, struck, demeaned, should be ashamed; no one who has lived together with the perpetrator should be ashamed; no one who lacked the courage to go straight to the police should be ashamed; no one should be ashamed of not having escaped more quickly or more radically from the sphere of violence or abused power. No one should be ashamed of having been unable to translate their shock immediately into fitting words, or having been unable to tell the story of a brutal rape in a perfect linear form, as if it was their most recent shopping list.

No one who repulses even minor annoyances should be ashamed; no one should be ashamed who protests against an unwanted hand on their body; no one who wants to decide for themselves when and where and with whom they go to bed should be ashamed; no one should be ashamed of having trusted a person or a situation that turned out to be dangerous; no one should be ashamed of someone else's behaviour.

No one should be shamed by another person's objectifying gaze; no one should be ashamed of their own pleasure, their own joy, their own clothes; no one should be accused of having allegedly wanted, allegedly provoked something they did not want; no one should be ashamed of their own body, their own desire, expressing their own conception of gender and sexuality, no matter whether that physicality, that sexuality, that expression of gender conforms to any tradition or norm.

Most bodies, most practices don't conform to any norm.
Deviation from the norm is much more widespread than the norm pretends.

Everyone should be able to discover and develop their own pleasure, in a language of their own, with their own body – and with the bodies and the pleasures of others. And no one should be ashamed of their own pleasure. As long as it includes the other person's pleasure – as long as the other person is an adult in a position to choose for themselves – everything that is arousing and pleasing is allowed.

*   *   *

Sometimes I'm in two minds whether I should be stating a demand for something so obvious. It is unpleasant to have to explain over and over again why human dignity is inviolable, to have to spell out over and over again what that dignity might be and who counts as human; it seems embarrassingly banal to have to explain why people deserve legal guarantees, why they must not be discriminated against just because they believe differently, love differently or have a different body than the majority expects; to have to explain over and over again why every person is entitled to decide what gives them pleasure, or why any person is entitled to be religious or trans or atheist. It is as humiliating as it is tiring to have to assert one's own rights and the rights of others over and over again.

Sometimes I feel as though criticizing inequality and discrimination must show a lack of imagination – after all, we're repeating what generations before us, with different experiences and different words, have already said. But an injustice is no less unjust simply because it has been around for a long time. Just because misogyny, just because racism, just because anti-Semitism have been handed down for generations and generations, they are no less illegitimate. The mere longevity of resentment and discrimination does not make them right. In that light, criticizing them is still, sadly, an urgent and a timely task.

Nevertheless, I am faced with the question how to articulate my own claims and protests, in what vocabulary, in what context; with what images and narratives I might persuade people who have not recognized them or taken them seriously up to now; with what language, with what gestures I can move people who don't want to be moved; with what philosophical acuity, what emotional weight, with what severity, what delicacy, what wit I can appeal to whom and open them to change? How is it possible to articulate the criticism of discrimination so that it feels right, yet not self-righteous? How is it possible to find the right balance: to be unyielding where I must but at the same time generous where I can? How is it possible to retain my scepticism of my own intuitions, to avoid making overquick, oversure moral judgements – and aesthetic judgements too for that matter?

Just as we need thick descriptions for a discerning analysis of individual cases, just as we need attention to the structures that are conducive to exclusion and inclusion, we also need flexible instruments that can be used to subvert or sanction practices and beliefs in the social and political sphere. When ironic subversion is more effective than sharp criticism, when prohibitions are really indispensable, and when open, contentious discussion is more productive – all this can be determined only case by case.

There are different forms of education, different means of prevention, of mediation, of regulation, of sanction of different kinds of abuse and contempt. Courts and prosecutors are responsible for some cases, but not for all. Subliminal, non-actionable forms of humiliation, habitual sexism, systematic discrimination call for a broad range of instruments.

What is clear is that we need more publicly supported spaces and accommodation for victims of domestic violence so that people are not compelled by a lack of living space to go on being abused month after month. On the one hand, that is simply a matter of spending the money to rent such spaces. But accommodation is not enough if the people there are not cared for by social workers or psychotherapists. Otherwise, such protection all too often gives the victims no more than a pause to catch their breath – and back they go into the affliction they just escaped. We also need shelters for men, ensuring that they are not blotted out as victims of sexualized violence. And we need unconditional protection for mistreated trans women, without telling them they are 'not female enough' for women's shelters.

We need greater sensitivity on the part of all those who have young people in their care, girls or boys: more mandatory seminars on sexualized violence in teacher training, and in the training of imams, rabbis, priests and ministers. We need independent agencies where victims can report assault without having to fear they will be rejected by an institution they are affiliated with, whether it is a church, a boarding school, or a research laboratory. We need more educational work in all kinds of communities on people's images of men, women and those in between or trans*, with decent respect, but without deference to taboos.

And, no matter how unimaginative it may seem in 2019 to have to explain the part about pay yet again: the gender pay gap needs to be closed. In the UK, it has changed little in the past decade, and in 2018 women earned on average 17.9 per cent less per hour than men.[11] That is not simply for lack of legal regulations: for years EU Directive 2006/54/EG has stipulated equal pay for men and women.[12] But women still tend to be working in lower-paid occupations; they are still misclassified within their companies; women are still not proportionately present in management positions.

We need more diversity in the boardrooms of leading companies, in the editorial offices of media concerns, in the artistic direction of theatres; we need more diversity in literature, in school textbooks, in the juries that decide who gets grants and scholarships, who directs plays and films, who writes screenplays – the list is long, and we need to make it longer and broader and deeper, over and over again. With each succeeding generation, in all different places with their own particular structures and practices of exclusion and discrimination.

Whether we achieve lasting change will depend mainly on whether the critique of sexism and abused power is able to address those social zones and life-worlds that are more precarious and marginalized. It is not enough to address sexual assault and harassment in artistic, academic and media contexts (although that is important). What matters just as much is the abuse of people who work in less visible, less stable jobs; what matters not least is women doing seasonal work in agriculture, women with precarious residence permits working as cleaners or housekeepers in the hotel industry, as waitresses in bars and pubs; what matters are refugee women (and young men) who are housed, alone or with their families, in arrival shelters, in containers or cell blocks with no locks on the showers; what matters are women whose dignity is denied to begin with, such as sex workers or prostitutes; what matters are women and men in prisons; what matters are people who cannot speak for themselves on their own, or to whom no one listens – older people in homes or in psychiatric wards; what matters are all those who live or work in places governed by strict hierarchies, where criticism is unwelcome or immediately punished.

Whether we achieve lasting change will also depend on perceiving men as well as women as potential victims of abuse and violence, not attaching attributes to images of men and women, not defining and ascribing what is supposed to be male or female. Lasting change will depend not least on whether we perceive and address men as allies. Whether we achieve lasting change will also depend on whether we can find a language that appeals to older people too, whether we can open up spaces in which encounters can take place; whether we achieve lasting change will also depend on whether we can always broaden the 'we' that I use here so casually, expand it again and again to appeal to more people with all kinds of different experiences.

* * *

In his memoir *Good Things Happen Slowly*, the jazz pianist Fred Hersch tells how long it took before he told his friends and colleagues, with whom he performed together night after night, that he was homosexual. He describes what prevented him from confiding in them: 'I had … always been afraid that straight musicians might not understand and that the music – and my reputation – would suffer as a result.' Hersch's worry that the music might suffer was linked to the special intimacy that arises through playing music together: 'When you're in a band, you fall in love with other musicians in a way. If you're a pianist, you may have found the perfect bass player, finally, or the drummer of your dreams. Musicians get musical crushes on one another … With this in mind, I thought the musicians

I was playing with might misconstrue that with me as a kind of come-on.'[13] That is all too famil- iar to most of us: the worry that others might feel uncomfortable simply by knowing about our homosexuality. Without making any kind of advance, we provoke awkwardness. To avoid frightening our heterosexual acquaintances (and sometimes even friends), we restrict ourselves, which can lead to misunderstanding. We censor our movements and our language, expurgating what we imagine others might imagine is inap- propriate. That can happen so intuitively that I no longer even notice it, no longer notice how strongly the habit inscribes in me the image of a toxic sexuality, how strongly the notion has become part of my own life that there might be something about me, that I might *be* something that scares people. I like to tell myself it is simply politeness, a sign of cautious empathy towards a heterosexual person – but what kind of an idea of homosexuals am I empathizing with?

Fred Hersch writes: 'At various times, certain jazz musicians who knew I was gay would say things like, "It's okay that you're gay. Just don't hit on me."'

That's just wonderful. Men who patronizingly claim to be unruffled by homosexuality in general but in the same breath need to prohibit being considered as an object of homosexual desire. That's really funny. Why do heterosexual men want to forestall having to react to another person's desire?

Women live with this situation constantly. Women are objects of other people's fantasies all the time. And there's nothing unbearable about it. Women are constantly being looked at and looked over, spoken to, more or less directly, more or less suavely – and have to react to it. They can engage with it and see what happens. Or they can ward it off, gracefully or bluntly, pleasantly or unpleasantly. But having to react to an offer they have no interest in is part of their day-to-day experience.

What exactly makes these men so anxious? Is it having to ward off someone's advances, and not knowing how? Is it having no practice at facing the unwanted lust of another person? Is it not knowing how multifaceted, how delicate, how complex it is to choose, from the repertoire of turndowns, one that is clear enough without being impolite or hurtful? Or to find, conversely, a rejection that is sufficiently friendly, but not so ambivalent that it could be reinterpreted as an invitation? Is it that they don't know that a whole art form is made up of the codes and norms that are constantly demanded of girls and women? That they don't know how to navigate this jungle of saying no without incurring danger, punishment, violence?

Or is the problem merely being looked at by a man? Is it being included in a homosexual fantasy that they, as heterosexuals, want no part of? Do they not understand the conventions of gay flirting? Does it upset them that they don't know how to interpret or use the gestures and glances? It's possible. But – couldn't they learn?

Or is what upsets them being looked at *at all*, having to imagine themselves as the addressee of another person's gaze? Is that what's so hard for them? Why? Is it because men, in the historical tradition of gender roles, have had the privilege of seeing themselves exclusively as subjects of desire? Is it because female pleasure, female desire, female subjectivity has been a kind of blank spot in the imagination? Or because sexuality is all too seldom imagined as mutual, as playful and open, as intersubjective and egalitarian?

That would be lovely: to break free of that one-sided, monological perspective. To engage with other people's gazes; to perceive that engagement as a space of possibility, as an open dialogue. To set ourselves in relation to another person and discover, together, what both people want, or don't want, as the case may be. Fred Hersch, by the way, writes that his musical expression grew deeper when he stopped concealing his sexuality. Perhaps the other musicians playing with him would also improve if they could relax and accept the possibility of being desirable to men.

*   *   *

If power doesn't operate only vertically – if power is something that arises whenever people connect and act in concert; if power denotes a potentiality – then that is what we should try to do: act together, look together for new perceptions, new concepts, new images, new languages, new forms of contact, of pleasure.

This too is power: searching together for more just forms of representation, participation, compensation, access, freedom and equality. This too is power: thinking of what we can do ourselves, remembering that there are others who have had the same experience, who can help; that we live under the rule of law, that there are people we can talk to in prosecutors' offices and in the police; that there are associations and groups offering advice and support.

This too is power: affirming that a legacy, a tradition, can be broken, that it doesn't have to go on being the way it's always been. This too is power: accepting other forms of family, ones that are able to support us, and laugh or mourn with us; being open to other forms of community, forms that don't exist yet, but that we discover together.

This too is power: charging into the open against repressive structures, against racist exclusion, against anti-Semitic resentments, against the stigmatization of people who believe differently, love differently, or live in different bodies than the norm prescribes.

This too is power: passing on the stories of those who have struggled for human rights and civil

rights before us, not forgetting them, but learning from them and branching out from them,
and also passing on the stories of those who have failed but who tried to work for finer, better forms of cooperation, and remembering the stories of the mothers and grandmothers who searched for themselves and their voices in more constricted spaces.

This too is power: taking seriously not just the experience of our elders but also that of younger people. Referring to those born later who are developing other concepts, other practices, that we can learn from.

This too is power: telling the stories of all the creative, civil, poetic forms of protest – they are the wellspring of political hope.

We shouldn't underestimate our own power; we shouldn't think of ourselves as defenceless, shouldn't let ourselves be isolated; we should look to each other, look for alliances, among friends, in families, at school, in the neighbourhood; allies with whom we can jointly break open the structures that permit violence and exploitation.

Power is still power.

It describes only possibilities.

It is the strength that allows a person to act and to speak, to change something; and it is the strength that can damage, maim, corrupt. Us, potentially. No one is entitled to think of themselves exclusively as powerless and innocent.

No background, no gender, no sexuality, no formerly fragile status is a safeguard against someday, somehow, thoughtlessly abusing the power one has.

In the end, it depends on how we want to use the spaces of desire. Whether we keep a critical eye on ourselves. Whether we manage to break up the new sedimentations before they harden; whether we manage to question the new certainties, who they benefit, what they cover up.

Because that is the challenge that remains: to stay alert to new, different mechanisms of exclusion and objectification. The lasting danger is that every emancipation overlooks its own contradictions and ambivalences, that we become blind to our own orthodoxies, the ones we unwittingly produce in our attempts to grow freer and more just.

*   *   *

In the beginning is doubt.
Before every sentence, every word, there is this threshold: Is that right? Is that correct? Besides being true, is it also truthful?
And those are just the doubts about *what* I might say.

I write as if I were mumbling: softly, more to myself than aloud for others to hear. Thinking, rather, but with a keyboard. Writing makes thinking more precise. It is intimate. Like whispering. Or like mumbling.

In the beginning is always doubt.
Sometimes I wish I could turn it off. But without these doubts we would no longer want to discover and touch others; we could no longer be curious to see what emerges when we encounter and desire one another.

Without doubt and careful listening,
without the dialogical perspective,

we wouldn't be able to learn,
wouldn't create pleasure,
wouldn't be ourselves.

Notes

1 Michel Foucault, '*Kenryoku to chi*' ['Pouvoir et savoir', 'Power and knowledge'], in *Dits et écrits*, vol. 2 (Paris: Gallimard, 2001). Interview with S. Hasumi, Paris, 13 October 1977.

2 Wendy Brown, 'Wounded attachments', *Political Theory* 21/3 (1993): 390–410.

3 Office for National Statistics, 'Domestic abuse in England and Wales: year ending March 2018', Appendix tables, www.ons.gov.uk/peoplepopulatio nandcommunity/crimeandjustice/bulletins/dome sticabuseinenglandandwales/yearendingmarch2018.

4 The most recent figures are for the year from April 2015 to March 2016. Office for National Statistics, 'Intimate personal violence and partner abuse', Appendix tables, www.ons.gov.uk/file?uri=/people populationandcommunity/crimeandjustice/datase

ts/appendixtablesfocusonviolentcrimeandsexualof
fences/yearendingmarch2016/fovappendixtablescor
rection22feb2018.xls.

5 Ibid.

6 Clifford Geertz refers to the term developed by
Gilbert Ryle, who also supplies the example. Clifford
Geertz, 'Thick description: towards an interpretive
theory of culture', in *The Interpretation of Cultures*
(New York: Basic Books, 1973), pp. 310–23.

7 Mesut Özil resigned from the German national
football team on 22 July 2018, citing discrimination
by the league president and racism in German society: 'I am German when we win, but an immigrant
when we lose' (https://twitter.com/MesutOzil1088/
status/1021093637411700741/photo/1). In the weeks
that followed, many Germans and immigrants to
Germany echoed his sentiments, marking their stories of discrimination with the hashtag #MeTwo.

8 Cf. 'Afghanistan's dancing boys', *BBC World
Service*, www.bbc.co.uk/programmes/poof0hh, and
'Baccha Baazi: Afghanistans Kinderprostituierte',
Welt,   www.welt.de/politik/ausland/article9189064/
Baccha-Baazi-Afghanistans-Kinderprostituierte.
html. For a very thorough study, with an impres-
sive analysis of those traditional forms of the 'boys'
play' that did not involve sexualized violence, see
Ingeborg Baldauf, *Die Knabenliebe in Mittelasien:
Bacabozlik*, n. p. [Berlin] 1988.

9 This section is based on one of my columns in the

Süddeutsche Zeitung: www.sueddeutsche.de/politik/kolumne-boeses-1.3028440.

10 The party AfD (*Alternative für Deutschland*, 'Alternative for Germany'), founded in 2013 as a Eurosceptic party, is a right-wing populist movement uniting ethnic-nationalist, anti-immigration, anti-feminist and historical revisionist currents.

11 See Office for National Statistics, 'Gender pay gap in the UK, 2018', www.ons.gov.uk/employmentandlabourmarket/peopleinwork/earningsandworkinghours/bulletins/genderpaygapintheuk/2018.

12 See National Archives, 'Directive 2006/54/EC of the European Parliament and of the Council', www.legislation.gov.uk/eudr/2006/54/contents.

13 Fred Hersch, *Good Things Happen Slowly: A Life in and out of Jazz* (New York: Crown Archetype, 2017), pp. 160–1.